Three Years

Amanda Caldwell

Presentation by *BookLeaf Publishing*

Web: www.bookleafpub.com

E-mail: info@bookleafpub.com

ISBN: 9789358316674

First edition 2023

To Henry and Khai, my endless source of inspiration

Poetry

Poetry has never been my thing
I was never any good at it anyway

How do you analyze a poem?
Break it down piece by piece?
Dissect each word and line
Until it lay before you a harmless
Corpse of meaning

But it isn't about facts and figures
A perfect equation to a perfect message

It's about feeling the words crash into you
Knock you over and pull you under
A rushing current
That only brings you back to the surface
Miles away from shore
Far away from the walls you've built up
And the safety net of analysis
Or the comfortable distance of intellectualization

Maybe I've always been afraid of poetry
Because I'm scared it will give me away

One Year

A year ago
I sat across from you
On a bench
A hot coffee
Warming my hands
From the winter chill
As we talked and talked
About all the things
We had missed
In each other's lives
Sharing old memories
And funny stories

Tonight
I sit next to you
On our couch
Your arm around me
As we cuddle
Under a blanket
To keep warm
During the winter nights
Making memories
We'll treasure
For a lifetime

The Spark

It always starts
With a spark

Every great piece of writing
Every war
Every revolution
Every great love

The spark that starts it all

An intense
Flash-bang
Of emotion and inspiration

But we started
With a smolder
A burning deep inside
That has been fanned
Into an intense flame

The Southern California Challenge

We started in the desert as the sun rose and the too-hot coffee burned our tongues. We followed the trails set out before us, winding through the open landscape, climbing the rocks that were twice our size. Laughing and full of energy and anticipation for the day ahead.

We went to the mountains, with snow under our feet and the sun high above us. We walked the streets of the small town, shoulder to shoulder, as we talked and talked, learning everything we could about each other.

We ended up at the beach, the sand between our toes as the sun hung low on the horizon. We climbed to the highest peak to sit and watch the last light of the day be swallowed by the gentle lapping of the ocean waves, silent and still as my hand rested on the bench next to yours.

Anxiety Thoughts

The thought comes
Like a worm in your ear
Burrowing into your brain
Growing roots
To stay anchored in place

Expanding

And

Expanding

Until it fills your mind
Until it's the only thing left
The thought that crept in
When you weren't looking
And is now the only thing
You can think

Afraid

I'm afraid to show you
The sides of me
That aren't pretty
Or perfect
Or flawless
The parts of me
That are splintered
And torn
And blemished
The emotions
And worries
That run so deep
I feel like I'm drowning

I'm afraid
You'll realize it's not enough
I'm not enough
That this isn't
What you signed up for

If I show you
This piece of me
Will you still stay?

Love and Anxiety

Everyone says
You get one
Great Love

That one person
Who understands you
Without words

And loves you
Unconditionally

The one who resonates
With your soul

And makes you happier
Than you've ever imagined

But no one tells you
How the anxiety stays with you

The worry and the fear
That creeps in at the strangest moments
Gripping your heart

And whispering in your ear

How easily this could all fade away

How one wrong move
Can turn your best days
Into your worst agony

How now that you have everything
You've ever wanted
You have so much to lose

And no one tells you
That it's okay to feel this way
That love does not make
The darkness disappear

But gives you a guiding light
And a hand to hold
As you continue to step forward
Trusting the path before you

The Dark Days

Most people think of depression
As the days when the dark swallows you up
Covers you in its sticky embrace
As you try to fight your way back to the light

When most of the time
You open your eyes in darkness
And try to remember
That the light exists

Rainstorm in a Drought

Your love came to me
Like a rainstorm in a drought
Filling the reservoir of emotions
Full to bursting
For the first time in years

When I Say I Love You - I

When I say
I love you
I love every piece of you

The pieces that are
Sharp and prickly
Honed to a razor's edge
By past experiences

The pieces that are
Heavy
And hard to hold
Laden with all the emotions
You haven't let go of

The pieces that are
Sticky
Gummy and viscous
With all the words
You've left unsaid

The pieces that are
Fragile and delicate
And might shatter
Into a million more

When I say
I love you
I love every piece of you

Two Years

You took me back to that beach
The one where we sat side by side
Two years ago
Letting the silence of what
We were too scared to say
Squeeze into the inches between us

You took me back to that beach
Maybe more nervous than before
Back to where we watched the sun
Sink behind the waves in silence

But this time our easy conversation
Swirled around us
The ring shining in the fading golden light
After I said yes

Happiness

Happiness is intimidating

A beautiful light
That embraces every
Part of you
In its warm glow

And exposes every
Piece of you
Like an x-ray
Searching for the
Places inside
That are the
Most vulnerable
And broken

Unsure and insecure
The fear that this feeling
Is only fleeting

The up
And up
And up

Like a rollercoaster
Before the big drop

I Think of You

As I lay in bed
Awake for the millionth time
I think of you

When I place my hand against my stomach
And feel you kick
I think of you

As I watch my body change
Growing to give you more space
I think of you

When I look down
And realize I can no longer see my feet
I think of you

Every time I feel you move
Twirling and kicking
I think of you

Even though we haven't met
I think of you
And I can't wait

Lifeblood

The blood of the Covenant
Is thicker than the water of the womb

Or so they say

But as you lay in my lap
Bundled from the cold
Snoring in peaceful slumber
I think about blood

My blood

The blood that runs through your veins
    And tints your cheeks a soft pink
The blood I saw
    The night before going to the hospital
The blood that gushed out
    After you were born
The blood in the plastic bag next to me
    Pumping back into my body
The blood I now see once a month
    That used to be an unwelcome sight
But is now a reminder that you are finally here
    In the world
And so am I

A Little Piece of Me

There's a little piece of me
When I look at his smile

There's a little piece of you
When I look into his eyes

He has my nose
And your chin

Like a jigsaw puzzle
Of our love

All the pieces shaken up
And rearranged
To create something new

The Things I Keep

"I am the place in which something has occurred."
-Claude Lévi-Strauss

They tell me to keep
His first outfit
A lock from his first haircut
An imprint of his little hands and feet
So I will always remember this time
And the tiny miracle I created

But I also keep
The scars from where the doctor
Stitched me up
A little extra around my waist
From my body nourishing yours
And the jagged purple lines
From where my skin stretched
To keep you safe

I keep the memories of you
Etched into my body
A reminder of the life that was made
And the bond that was created
Forever

When I Say I Love You - II

When I say I love you
I love every part of you

I love your little toes
And the way you curl them
When we tickle the bottom of your feet

I love your eyes
The deep brown
That reminds me so much of your dad

I love your smile
And the way you
Wait for us to return it

I love your giggle
And your little babbles
As you tell me about your day

I love watching you get bigger
Your unique personality
Shining through more every day

When I say I love you
I love getting to love
Every new part of you

The Art of Love

The art of love is
Abstract and hard to pin down
Full of the unexpected
Like Picasso

Raw and real
Exposing the vulnerable
Like Johannes Vermeer

Soft and colorful
Simple in its expression
Like Georgia O'Keeffe

Wild and crazy
And full of imagination
Like Salvador Dali

Sweet and delicate
Cherishing the little moments
Like Monet

Muted yet magical
Distinctive in its expression
Like Charles Rennie Mackintosh

Honest and unassuming
But layered with meaning
Like Frida Kahlo

Quiet and understanding
Focused on the experience
Like Bob Ross

Messy and untamed
And hard to explain
Like Jackson Pollock

But mostly the art of love is
Uniquely beautiful
Always finding magic in the ordinary
Like Vincent Van Gogh

Three Years

Time is a funny thing
The way it ebbs and flows
    It can rush like rapids
    Or be a lazy river ride

First you track it by the lines on the wall
And then the lines on your face
    The change that proves time is moving
    The new turning old until old is new

It didn't seem like much at the time
One message with a simple question
But then you add three years
    A time skip
A jump to a point that seemed so impossible
    But now feels so inevitable

A kiss
    That caught me off guard
    But lingered on my lips

A ring on my finger
    A physical reminder of our love
    That shines with all our promises

Our son

Nestled between us
With my smile and your dimples

A simple message with a question
That didn't seem like much
But that's what's funny about time

Enough

I don't know how to do this
This giving up of myself
Putting everything on the page
Exposing myself so intimately to another
Opening up the parts of myself
That I'm most unsure of
Sharing the thoughts I'm most scared of

And hoping
Hoping it is enough
Hoping this is enough
Hoping I am enough

I don't know how to do this
But I promised myself I would try
And that is enough

Milton Keynes UK
Ingram Content Group UK Ltd.
UKHW012311160324
439511UK00013B/347